I Need a Friend

I Talk You Talk Press

CONTENTS

CHAPTER ONE

Apartment 3
205 Rue d'Auberge
Paris
May 20, 2017

Dear Rosie,

If you get this letter, I know you will be surprised. I don't know where you are living now. Are you married? Do you have a new name? I looked for you on the Internet, and on Facebook, but I couldn't find you. So I am sending this letter to your parents' address. I hope that somehow you will receive it.

Do you remember when we were best friends? We met at school when we were eight. The last time I saw you, we were both fifteen years old. My parents were getting a divorce, and my mother was going to stay with her family in Ireland. I had to go with her. My father was gone, and I was losing my best friend. I was going to live in a new country. I didn't know anyone in Ireland. I would be going to a new school among strangers. I was so unhappy. I was frightened too.

I promised I would send you the address when we found somewhere to live in Ireland. I promised I would write to you. I promised I would call you. My mother said I could come back and visit you. What happened? Why didn't I write to you? Why didn't I come back to visit you? It's hard to remember, but I think I was angry with you. I know I was jealous. You had a brother, two parents, a dog, a house and a beautiful garden. My mother and I were sharing a bedroom in a horrible dark house in Cork. We were living with her sister and her husband.

1

They didn't want us there.

It was a long time ago and of course our lives are different now. I am living in Paris. It is such a beautiful and exciting city. I work for a fashion magazine. I love my job. I often get free clothes and cosmetics. Have you ever been to Paris? I am sure you have. I hope you might come and stay with me. It would be wonderful to meet again. You can tell me about your life. We can talk about our childhood. We can look at the old photographs and laugh. It would be wonderful. I know the first weekend in June is a holiday weekend in England. Maybe if you are not doing anything you could come then.

Of course you might have a husband and two children. Maybe you don't even live in England any more. Maybe you won't get this letter. But if you do get it, - if you can come – please, please do.

Love from your one-time best friend,
Shelley

CHAPTER TWO

Rosemary sat at her kitchen table and stared at the letter. It was typed. She picked up the envelope. The address was written in pencil. The letter had been posted in Paris on May 20th. It had been delivered to her parents' old house in Cheltenham. Someone had crossed out the address and written the address of Rosemary's apartment on the envelope. It had been delivered today, June 1st.

Three years ago, her parents sold their house to a friend of Rosemary's brother. They were living in Spain now.

My brother's friend, Jeremy, must have called my brother, thought Rosemary. *That's how he got my address.*

Rosemary remembered when Shelley left Cheltenham. Shelley had cried all the time. She didn't want to leave, and she was missing her father. Rosemary and her mother went to visit Shelley's mother. Rosemary's mother wanted to help, but Shelley's mother wouldn't talk to anyone. She was packing suitcases. She was banging doors and throwing things. Rosemary thought about Shelley's father. He was a very quiet man who worked as a postman. One day he came home from work and said he was leaving. He had met a very beautiful Chinese woman. She was only 22. He was going to live with her in Hong Kong. He planned to get a job as a teacher in a language school. Two days later, he was gone. Two weeks after that, Rosemary stood on the platform of the railway station, waving as the train with Shelley and her mother on board pulled out of the station.

I waited and waited for a letter from Shelley, thought Rosemary. *I couldn't understand why she didn't contact me. She was my best friend and she hurt me so much.*

After six months Rosemary accepted that Shelly was gone from her life. She realized that she would not get a letter or a phone call. Shelley would not come to visit. She made new friends, studied for her GCSEs and A levels, went to university, and then got a job in a library in London. And now this. A letter from the past.

Rosemary got up from the table and went to the bookshelf in her living room. She pulled out a photograph album and took it back to the kitchen. She slowly turned the pages. There were family groups from Christmas and birthdays, and school photographs. There were no photographs of Shelley until Rosemary was eight. After that it seemed that Shelley was in almost every photograph. Rosemary and Shelley on the swing in the garden. Rosemary and Shelley at ballet class. Rosemary and Shelley with their families at a restaurant. *What celebration was that?* Rosemary couldn't remember.

The last photograph in the album was of Rosemary and Shelley outside Rosemary's parents' house. It was the day before Shelley left. Rosemary's father had taken it. The girls had their arms around each other. Small dark-haired Shelley, and tall blonde Rosemary.

I wonder why it's the last photograph in the album? thought Rosemary. *I guess we got digital cameras about that time. So all the later photographs are on the computer.*

That gave Rosemary an idea. She made herself a cup of tea. Then she took her laptop from her briefcase and turned it on. *I'll search the Internet for Shelley.*

Twenty minutes later, Rosemary gave up. She had searched all the online social media, records in Ireland, and fashion magazines in Paris. Shelley's father had been killed in a car accident in Hong Kong only six months after he had left England. She found that Shelley's mother had died five years previously. But there was no record of Shelley anywhere.

Rosemary shivered. It was cold in the apartment. She had picked up the letter from her mailbox and read it as soon as she came in from work. That was more than an hour ago. She turned on the heaters and went to her bedroom to change out of her work clothes. She switched on the television and took some soup out of the refrigerator. Sitting in front of the television with her soup, cheese and crackers, Rosemary wondered what she was going to do. Her thoughts were racing.

Why did Shelley contact me now? Maybe I could ask her? But there is no email address and no telephone number in the letter. Maybe she wants to see me because her life is so good. She wants to share her life with me. What should I do? I can ignore the letter, or I can go to Paris. Why should I go? She wants me to visit this weekend. Today is Friday.

Rosemary knew that she would go to Paris. She knew that she had to go. Shelley was not her friend now. But long ago they had been best friends. And at the bottom of the letter, in pencil, Shelley had written, *I need a friend very badly. Please come.*

CHAPTER THREE

Early the next morning, Rosemary sipped a cup of coffee as she stared out of the plane window.

I'm crazy, she thought. *Why am I doing this? I'll go to see Shelley. Maybe we can have a cup of coffee, or even lunch. And then I'll tell her I have things to do, and people to see. I'll book into a good hotel and have a lovely weekend in Paris, all by myself.*

At Charles de Gaulle airport, Rosemary showed the address on Shelley's letter to the man at the information counter.

"You can take a train to Gare du Nord," said the man. "Then the Metro to Réaumur – Sébastopol. It's about 10 minutes' walk from there to that address."

It was a beautiful spring day in Paris, and Rosemary enjoyed the journey very much. She had been to Paris with her parents twice and once with some friends from the library.

Shelley thought I might be married with children. I date a lot, but I never seem to meet someone I want to stay with. Perhaps Shelley will have some advice for me. Or maybe she knows some handsome Frenchman she can introduce me to.... Rosemary realized she was looking forward to seeing Shelley. *I haven't had a very close girlfriend to talk to, and to laugh with, since Shelley. We used to tell each other everything – it would be nice to talk about my love life with her.*

Rosemary had a small suitcase on wheels and a shoulder bag. It was easy to walk from the Metro Station to Rue d'Auberge.

She was surprised when she found the street number. It was on a big wooden gate with tall stone fences on either side. She looked through a gap in the gate. Behind the fence was a courtyard filled with garbage cans and bicycles. There were two old trees. Piles of old newspapers and cardboard wine boxes were stacked against the walls of a three-storey building at the back of the courtyard. It looked poor and dirty.

I thought Shelley would live in some amazing modern building. Maybe a very small apartment, but very smart and chic. Or maybe in one of those amazing beautiful buildings from the 18th century. The ones with chandeliers and tall narrow windows. This looks like an apartment building for poor people, or very old people. Shelley works for a fashion magazine. Why would she live here?

Rosemary checked the street number again. It was the right number. She tried to open the gate, but it was locked. Then she saw a rusty grill with a white intercom button and a dirty piece of cardboard with the word "Concierge" printed on it.

Concierge is the French word for the apartment manager, thought Rosemary. *I can push the button and ask for Shelley. I hope the concierge speaks English. I only know about twenty words of French.*

She pushed the button and waited. Nothing happened. She pushed the button again. This time a crackling noise came from the grill and she heard, "Qu'est-ce que vous voulez?"

That means 'What do you want?' thought Rosemary.

"I want to visit Shelley White. Umm - Je veux visiter Shelley White."

"Eh?"

"I want to visit Shelley White", Rosemary said loudly. "Je veux visiter Shelley White."

"Shelley White n'est pas là," answered the voice.

"What do you mean, she isn't there? Sorry! Mais…"

There was a click and then silence. Rosemary stood and stared at the gate. *Perhaps Shelley is out. She didn't know I was coming. I'll go and have some lunch somewhere and come back.*

She pulled her suitcase along the street and looked for somewhere to eat lunch. On the corner she found a café with tables outside. Rosemary sat at one of them and wondered why she had come to Paris. She felt tired and confused. The waiter came, and she looked at the menu. She ordered a ham sandwich and a coffee.

While she was waiting for her order, Rosemary took Shelley's letter out of her shoulder bag and read it again. *Why did Shelley write to me? Why did I come here?*

It was a quiet street, and the café was not busy. There were six tables outside on the street, but only one other table had a customer. A man was sitting looking at a laptop screen. Rosemary looked at him and then looked away – she wasn't interested in meeting men. Well, not today. She just wanted to meet Shelley, have a quick meeting with her, and escape somewhere nice for the rest of the weekend.

When the waiter came out with Rosemary's order, the man at the other table looked up. He signalled to the waiter, and ordered another coffee. As he did so, he saw Rosemary. He stared at her. Just for a moment, then he looked back at his computer screen. But the waiter was old and very experienced.

Oh, thought the waiter. *He is interested. Of course. She is a very beautiful woman. So tall, so blonde, so English. The beautiful blue eyes. The long thin fingers. He likes her.*

The old man smiled as he went back into the restaurant.

Rosemary finished her sandwich quickly.

I was hungry, she thought. *That's why I was feeling so worried.*

She drank her coffee slowly. She watched the people in the street. It was not a place for tourists. It was just a quiet part of the city where people lived normal lives. She watched the mothers pushing small children in strollers. An old man and woman walked past holding hands. Two young people pulled up on a motorcycle, and shouted to someone in the restaurant. A young waiter wearing a white apron came out and talked to them. It seemed they were making a plan for a party.

After an hour, Rosemary went inside the café and paid her bill. She came out and walked back down the street to Shelley's apartment building. She didn't notice that the man from the other table outside the café had left a pile of euros on his table, and was following her.

CHAPTER FOUR

Rosemary stopped outside the gate and pushed the button next to the sign that said concierge. It was the same conversation as before.

"Qu'est-ce que vous voulez?" What do you want?

I want to visit Shelley White. "Je veux visiter Shelley White."

"Shelley White n'est pas là." Shelley White is not here.

Rosemary sighed. *I give up. I'll go back to Gare du Nord and find a hotel.*

"Can I help you?"

Rosemary jumped. "Sorry," said the man. "Can I help you?"

There was a man standing behind her.

"Do you want to get in?" asked the man.

That's the man who was at the café, thought Rosemary.

Rosemary stared at him. He spoke like an Englishman. He was very good looking. He was very tall and he had dark hair and dark brown eyes. He smiled. "Sorry. I don't want to interfere. But you seem to have a problem. Maybe I can help."

"I came to stay with my friend. She lives in that building." Rosemary pointed to the building behind the wall. "But the concierge says she is not here. I can't get in."

"What is your friend's name?" asked the man.

"Uh, Shelley White," answered Rosemary.

"OK," said the man. "Shall I try?"

Rosemary stood back, and the man pushed the button. When the concierge said 'Qu'est-ce que vous voulez?' the man answered in French. He spoke very quickly, and Rosemary could not understand. But there was a loud click and a noise, and the gate opened.

"Thank you," said Rosemary. "Your French is very good!"

She smiled at the man and walked through the open gate. She thought that the man would say, 'You're welcome,' and go away. But he didn't. He walked through the gateway and said, "Now we need to find your friend."

"Oh no!" said Rosemary. "You have been very kind. I will be OK."

The man smiled. "You have to talk to the concierge. I don't think your French is good enough. Let me help you."

He reached over and took the handle of Rosemary's suitcase. He walked towards the building pulling her suitcase. Rosemary felt angry, but she followed him to a door almost hidden behind the boxes of empty wine bottles. There was a sign above the door. It said 'Concierge'. The man stopped in front of the door and smiled at her. "My name's Adam," he said. "And you are?"

"Rosemary," she answered but she felt very angry. This man was taking control, and she didn't like it.

He opened the door and shouted "Service!" He turned to Rosemary. "What number is your friend's apartment?"

An old and fat woman appeared. Before the concierge could say anything, Adam started talking. They talked for several minutes. The concierge looked angry and then, after Adam talked some more, she seemed to calm down. She even smiled. Adam turned to Rosemary, "Your friend is not here. But if you are invited as a guest, she will open the apartment for you. Do you have anything to show your friend invited you?"

I'm crazy, thought Rosemary. *But everything about this situation is crazy.*

Slowly she opened her shoulder bag and gave Adam the letter. He glanced at the letter, and then turned back to the concierge. The concierge shrugged. She went back into her room and came out with two keys on a ring.

Adam turned to Rosemary and smiled. "I told her you were invited. She will open the apartment for you."

"Thank you," said Rosemary. "I will be OK now."

"But I want to make sure everything is OK. I will come with you," said Adam.

"Just give me the key, and tell me where the apartment it is," Rosemary said loudly.

Adam took her arm and pointed to the main door of the building.

"It's on the second floor."

Rosemary picked up her suitcase. The ground was too rough to wheel it. She started walking towards the main door of the apartment building. Her suitcase felt heavy.

It would be nice if Adam would carry it for me, she thought. *He hasn't given me the apartment keys!* She looked back. Adam was giving something to the concierge. Rosemary couldn't see what it was, but perhaps it was money.

Adam smiled and came walking after her. "I'll show you the way," he said. He walked past Rosemary, and up the steps to the main door. He opened the door with one of the keys and left it open for Rosemary. He went on ahead up the stairs, leaving Rosemary to carry her suitcase.

I don't want him here. But if he won't go away, he could at least carry my suitcase, she thought.

On the second floor, the door to the apartment was open. Rosemary walked into a small entrance hall. From there she could see into a living room. She left her suitcase in the hall and went in. The curtains were half-closed and the room was dark. The ceiling was low. Rosemary looked around. The room smelt damp and dusty. The furniture was dark and heavy. There were ornaments and pictures and photographs everywhere.

This is an old person's room, thought Rosemary. *Why is Shelley living here? Maybe she hasn't had time to redecorate.*

Just then Adam came back. "There's no one here," he said.

"Of course not!" said Rosemary. "It's Shelley's apartment, and she is not here. I guess she will come back soon."

Adam looked at her strangely. He opened his mouth. Rosemary thought he was going to say something, but he didn't. He looked at her.

"You have been very helpful and I am very grateful," said Rosemary. "But now I am going to take a shower, get changed and wait for my friend to come home."

"I can stay with you until she comes," said Adam.

"No thank you." Rosemary thought Adam was very strange. She thought he might be dangerous. "Please go."

"OK," said Adam. "If you have any trouble with the concierge, just call me." He took a notebook out of his pocket and pulled a page out. He wrote a phone number on it. He put out his hand to give it to Rosemary, but she didn't take it. Adam shrugged. He folded the page in half and dropped it into her shoulder bag. "It's there if you want to call. You can call anytime."

Rosemary was still nervous about Adam. "Do you live near here?"

He said, "I'm sure I'll be around." He smiled at her. He went out the door, and down the stairs. Rosemary hurried to a window and pulled the curtains open. She watched Adam walk across the courtyard and out the gate.

Thank goodness he's gone, she thought. *I suppose he was helpful but he was making me nervous.*

CHAPTER FIVE

Rosemary opened all the curtains in the living room. The spring sun made the room brighter, but it made it look worse. She tried to open a window but none of them would open. Everything was dusty. She checked that the door was locked, and carried her suitcase back into the living room. She took out some clean clothes and looked for the bathroom.

The bathroom was very small and dirty. Rosemary turned on the light switch but nothing happened.

Perhaps the bulb is broken, she thought. There was a red toothbrush on the edge of the basin and a small tube of toothpaste. The towel on the towel rack was very old and smelt of mould. Rosemary went back to her suitcase and took out a small hand towel.

I will have to use this. I don't want to search through Shelley's closets to find a towel.

Rosemary turned on the water for the shower. She waited a long time, but the water was still cold. She looked around the walls of the bathroom and found an electric water heater. There were no lights on the control panel.

What is wrong? she asked herself. She went into the kitchen, the bedroom and the living room. She tried all the light switches. Nothing. There was no electricity.

Back in the living room, Rosemary threw her clean clothes back in her suitcase and sat down on one of the old dusty sofas. She stared at an old-fashioned desk with a very old-style typewriter on it.

Where's her computer? Shelley can't be living here! I must be in the wrong apartment! What number is this apartment?

She went out to the hall, unlocked the door and looked at the number on the door. The number was 3.

I am sure Shelley's letter said Apartment 3. I should check. Rosemary took her shoulder bag and looked for the letter. It wasn't there. *I gave it to that horrible man when he was talking to the concierge! He didn't give it back to me! Now what am I going to do? I don't know what he said to the concierge. He spoke so quickly, and my French is so bad.* Then she remembered. *He took the key with him as well! I can't go out. If I go out I can't come back in.* Rosemary thought that was a good idea. *I can go out of here with my suitcase, and forget I ever came here. This must be the wrong apartment. If I look around, maybe I can find out who lives here. I am sure no one has been here for a while. Maybe the person who lives here is away on holiday.*

Rosemary saw a door in the living room. She opened the door and went in. It was a bedroom. The room was very dark. She went to the window and pulled the curtains. It wasn't a window. It was a glass door. It opened onto a tiny balcony. She tried the door and it opened. Rosemary didn't close the door.

The fresh air will come in and that will make the room smell better, she thought. She turned and looked around the room. There was a big old bed but there were no sheets or blankets on it. She looked in the heavy wooden closet – there were a lot of old clothes. The kind of clothes an old lady might wear. A black coat, an old fur coat, some dresses.

She looked in the drawers of the dressing table. There were piles of underwear but none of them looked like a young woman's clothes. In the top drawer was a shiny black jewellery box. Rosemary felt bad about opening it, but she had to know. Was this really Shelley's apartment? Or someone else's?

She opened the jewellery box, but it was empty.

Just then a mouse ran across the room. Rosemary screamed and dropped the box.

When she stopped shaking, she knelt down to pick up the box.

I'll put this back and then I'm leaving! This isn't Shelley's apartment. I made a mistake. I'll call Adam and get the letter back, and find out where Shelley lives. Maybe this isn't even the right building! Or even the right street! Shelley will laugh when I tell her about this.

As Rosemary picked up the box, she saw a backpack under the bed. She stood up very carefully, put the box back in the drawer, and closed it.

Then very slowly, she knelt down and took the backpack from under the bed. She put it on the bed and looked at it. She had seen the backpack before.

When Rosemary and Shelley were fourteen, they had gone on a school camping trip. Rosemary's parents gave her a backpack for her birthday. Shelley didn't have one. Evan, Rosemary's brother, was going to university. Their parents bought him a new backpack. They gave Evan's old backpack to Shelley.

Eleven years later, Rosemary was standing in a strange apartment in Paris. An apartment, that probably belonged to an old lady. She was staring at a blue backpack with the name Evan Moulton written in marker pen on the front pocket.

Rosemary picked up the backpack, and threw it under the bed. She ran out of the bedroom and closed the door behind her. She leaned against the bedroom door and tried to calm down.

Shelley is here! What is going on? She works for a fashion magazine. Why is she living in this terrible, old dirty apartment? There is no electricity! It is filled with someone else's things!

After a while, Rosemary started to feel better. *Maybe Shelley was staying here for a while. Maybe she moved out to a new apartment, and forgot to take the backpack with her.*

She probably has beautiful suitcases, and forgot about that dirty old bag. But why did she give me this address? In the letter she said she didn't contact me from Ireland because she was angry with me. She said when she was fifteen years old, she was jealous of me. Maybe she is still angry. Maybe this is a cruel joke. She will arrive here laughing. She will tell me she wanted to tease me.

Rosemary went into the tiny kitchen and got a glass of water. She went back into the living room and found a magazine in her shoulder bag. She sat on the sofa near the window and waited for Shelley to come.

After a while, the magazine fell to the floor. Rosemary put her head against the dusty sofa cushion and fell asleep.

CHAPTER SIX

Rosemary woke up suddenly. She felt frightened. It was very late. The room was very dark.

Where am I? Then she remembered.

There was a noise. That must be Shelley.

She opened her mouth to call out and then she stopped. Something was making her feel very nervous. Something was wrong. She sat very still and listened. There was a scratching noise from the front hall. Someone was trying to open the door.

If it's Shelley, she will have a key! Adam has a key too! So it's not him! Who is it? I must hide. I am so frightened!

She reached down and found her shoulder bag. It was on the floor next to her feet. Then without breathing, she stood up and crept across the room to the bedroom door. She opened it as quietly as she could.

I didn't shut the door to the balcony. I can hide there, she thought. Rosemary walked quietly across the room. She was praying she didn't bang into anything. When she got to the glass door, she slipped through and pulled the curtains behind her. The door had a handle on the outside and she could close it.

On the balcony, Rosemary sat with her back against the wall, until she stopped shaking.

What am I going to do? Call the police? I can't do that. I don't know who is in the apartment. Maybe it is the owner. I will probably be arrested for being here. But I have to do something!

She stood up and put her ear against the door. She couldn't hear anything. Then she saw a light through the gap in the curtains. Someone was moving around with a torch. She could see the beam of light bouncing up and down.

I don't care if the police arrest me. Being in a police station would be better than this! She put her hand into her shoulder bag to find her phone. Her fingers closed on a piece of paper. It was the telephone number Adam had written down for her. Suddenly, being with Adam seemed to be much safer.

He has the key from the concierge and he would have called out. It's not him in there with the torch. He's English too. And he speaks such good French. He could call the police for me. He could explain.

Rosemary bent over her phone and punched in the number on the card.

Adam answered very quickly.

"Yes?"

"Adam. It's Rosemary! Shelley hasn't come back and there's someone in the apartment!"

"Where are you?"

"I'm on the balcony. It is outside the bedroom."

"OK. Don't move. Don't do anything. I will be there soon."

He hung up and Rosemary waited. She looked across the courtyard to the gate. She couldn't see anyone. It was very dark. There was a streetlight just outside the gate and she could see a faint pool of light on the stones of the courtyard. She thought it probably came from the concierge's room. She looked at her phone. It was almost midnight.

Then there was a lot of noise in the apartment. She heard men shouting and a bang – it sounded like a piece of furniture had fallen over. Next, she heard the sound of breaking glass. Someone came running into the bedroom. Rosemary pushed herself against the wall. She was terrified. The door opened and she screamed.

"It's OK, Rosemary," said Adam. "It's me."

Rosemary threw herself towards Adam and burst into tears.

Adam put his arms around her. "It's OK. You're safe now."

He stroked her hair and rubbed her back until she stopped crying. Then he took his jacket off and wrapped it around her. "It would be a good idea if you stay here until they have gone."

Rosemary looked at him. "Who are they?"

"They are special policemen. They know you are here, but they don't want anyone to see you. So just stay here, and be very quiet."

He smiled at her. He put his fingers to his lips to tell her to be quiet, and then he was gone.

It was fifteen minutes before he came back. Rosemary had stopped thinking of Adam as a very nice safe man. She was angry with him again. She was cold and tired.

Who does he think he is? He took my letter. He took the key away with him. He told me to stay out here and not make any noise!

Adam came back and said, "You can come in now."

Rosemary looked at him angrily. "Thank you!" she shouted. Adam laughed and Rosemary wanted to hit him.

She walked past him and into the living room. The room was empty. A table had been knocked over and some ornaments were broken. Rosemary's water glass was on the floor. Then she noticed the lights were on. This made Rosemary cross too. She couldn't find a way to get electricity, but Adam had.

"Where was the switch for the electricity?" she asked. "I couldn't find it."

"The electricity was turned off by the electricity company. We asked them to turn it back on. "

"In the middle of night?"

"We have powerful friends," answered Adam. He was laughing.

"What's so funny?" asked Rosemary.

"You were in terrible danger. You might have been killed. But all you want to talk about is the electricity!"

Rosemary sat down quickly on a sofa. She pulled Adam's leather jacket around her shoulders. She stared at him.

"What's happening?"

Adam sat down next to her. "It's a long story. I'll tell you a little, and then, I'm sorry, but there is something I have to ask you to do. After that I'll take you to a hotel. You can't stay here."

"But what if Shelley comes back?"

"Shelley won't come back here," said Adam quietly.

"But her bag is here. I found it. But maybe she has moved to a new apartment and just forgot it...."

Adam put his finger very softly on Rosemary's lips and she stopped talking.

"We'll talk about Shelley in a minute. First, I want to tell you who I am. I am a policeman. I work with the drug squad in London. I grew up in France, so my French is good. When the British police and the French police are working together, they like me to be part of the team. The man who came here tonight was looking for drugs. He didn't find any. He had two friends waiting outside. So we caught three members of the gang. It was a success."

"How did you get here so quickly? I called you, and you arrived in about two minutes."

"I was waiting very close by with members of the Paris drug squad. We thought the gang might try something tonight."

"Why tonight?" asked Rosemary.

Adam looked down at the floor. "Because you were here. The French police thought maybe you were carrying drugs or maybe had come here to collect them. The gang are looking for the drugs too."

Rosemary stood up. She took off Adam's jacket and threw it at him.

"You took the keys away so I wouldn't leave! You knew I could be in danger! You are a rat!"

Adam nodded. "I felt like a rat. I didn't think you had anything to do with drugs, but I wasn't sure. When I saw you at the café, I recognised you."

"Me? You never saw me before!" Rosemary was still very angry.

Adam sighed. "Please sit down."

Rosemary sat down as far away from Adam as she could. "OK. I'm listening. Explain."

"Two days ago, the French police found a woman's bag down by the river. It had a drugs and needles in it. There was also a purse with a little money, and there was this photograph. When I saw you at the café, even though you are older now, I knew you were the girl in the photograph."

He picked his jacket up from the floor and took a piece of paper from one of the pockets. He handed it to Rosemary. She stared at it. It was a photocopy of a photograph. The same photograph Rosemary had looked at in the album in her apartment. The last photo in the album.

"It's Shelley and me. My father took it. We were fifteen. It was the day before she went to Ireland with her mother. He got the film developed, and gave me two copies. One for Shelley, and one for me. I gave this to her the next day at the railway station. I never saw her again."

"I'm sorry," said Adam. "The French police found out that the photograph was taken in England. They asked me to come to Paris. We knew that drugs were coming into this area of Paris. We knew someone was buying and selling drugs near here. But we didn't know anything else. I was spending time in cafes and on the streets. I thought maybe I would see something useful. Do you remember the young couple on the motorbike that stopped outside the café?"

"Yes, I do," answered Rosemary. "They shouted, and the young waiter came out to talk to them."

"I thought they might be doing a drug deal. Then I saw you! I couldn't believe it!".

"So you followed me."

"Yes, I followed you. I got you into the apartment. I had to give the concierge money to give me the key. Then I planned to wait and see what happened. But you made me go away, and I didn't want you to know I was a policeman. But I had your name and address, and the letter. The police in England checked up on you. Everyone is happy now. I don't think you have anything to do with drugs."

There was a long silence.

"So is this Shelley's apartment?" asked Rosemary.

"No. It belonged to a very old lady who died about three months ago. It belongs to her nephew now. He lives in the South of France, and has not come to empty it out yet. He arranged to have the electricity and gas shut off, and that was all. Of course the concierge knew that. So I had to give her a lot of money to give me the key."

"So why was Shelley's bag here? Why did she give me this address?"

"I think she needed somewhere to live. Maybe she needed somewhere to hide. She must have found out this apartment was empty and moved in. I don't know where she found a key. Maybe the old lady hid one under the mat or something."

Rosemary sat very quietly. She didn't say anything.

"Rosemary?" Adam was worried. "Are you OK?"

"I guess I am still very confused. And I'm very tired and hungry. But where is Shelley? Do you think she will come back here?"

"No. She won't come back here. Do you remember I said there was something I must ask you to do?"

"Yes," said Rosemary quietly. "But I don't understand."

"Come on. Let's go. I'll find you something to eat." Adam stood up. He took Rosemary's suitcase and closed it. He took Rosemary's hand and pulled her to her feet.

CHAPTER SEVEN

Adam had a car and driver waiting out on the street. They went first to a large building on Ile de la Cité. The car pulled into a car park.

"Stay here," said Adam.

Rosemary waited with the silent driver until Adam came back with a paper cup of coffee and a cheese sandwich.

"Here," he said. "Have these. I got them from the cafeteria. I need to talk to some people, but I won't be long."

Rosemary was cold and hungry. She drank the coffee and ate the sandwich. Adam came back with another man.

"This is Henri," he said.

Henri got in the front of the car next to the driver and Adam sat in the back seat of the car next to Rosemary. "Place Marzas," Henri said to the driver.

The driver drove over the bridge and along the Seine. He pulled into a car park near a large red brick building. Rosemary looked at the sign on the building. 'Institute Medico-Legale.'

"What are we doing here?"

Adam held Rosemary's hand and said, "This morning, some joggers found the dead body of a young woman on the banks of the Seine. It was close to where the bag with the photograph was found. We think it might be Shelley. Could you look at the body? Maybe you can tell us if it's Shelley."

Rosemary felt sick. "I don't know. I guess so."

"I'll be with you all the time. It will be OK. I know you are strong enough to do this."

Rosemary didn't feel strong at all. But she got out of the car and she and Adam followed the man called Henri into the building.

"Who is he?" whispered Rosemary nodding towards Henri. "Why is he here?"

"I am only a guest of the French Police. Henri is the detective in charge of finding out who the young woman is, and what happened to her. He has to be here."

Henri spoke to the man on the front desk. Then the three of them walked down a long narrow corridor. It was very quiet. There seemed to be no one else in the building.

It's 1:30 am on a Sunday. Of course no one's working. Only the people who have to, thought Rosemary. They passed laboratories and offices until they came to an open door. Inside, the room looked like a waiting room. There were small sofas and comfortable chairs. Rosemary saw a water cooler, and a coffee table, with a box of tissues on it.

"Sit down," said Adam. "They will be ready for you soon."

Rosemary sat down. Adam stood behind her, his hand on the back of Rosemary's chair. She watched Henri walk through a door on the far side of the room. Very soon he came back. "She is ready," he said to Rosemary. "Can you come now?"

Adam and Henri walked each side of her as she went into the next room. There was an older woman with a kind face standing next to a narrow table. She pulled back the cloth covering the body just a little, so Rosemary could see a head, but no more.

"What do you think, Rosemary?" asked Adam. "Is that Shelley?"

Rosemary looked. The face was white and small. The hair was bright pink. There were many earrings in the ears and another earring in the nose. Maybe it was Shelley, but Rosemary hoped it wasn't. She hoped that somehow this was all a terrible dream and she would wake up.

She looked hard. "I don't know. I last saw her ten years ago. I am not sure."

Adam touched her back. "It's OK. We hoped you would know, but if you are not sure…"

"Can I see her right arm?" asked Rosemary.

The woman with the kind face looked at Rosemary. "Are you sure?" she asked.

"Yes," said Rosemary. "If it is Shelley, she will have a scar near her elbow."

The woman pulled the cloth off the tiny dead body. Rosemary leaned over. Just by the elbow there was a bright pink scar. It was shaped like a V.

Rosemary sighed. "It's Shelley," she said. Then she stared at the thin white arm. It was covered with red lines and red marks.

"Shelley! Drugs!" Rosemary felt dizzy. Adam took her arm and pulled her out of the room. He pushed her down onto one of the chairs. He knelt on the floor next to her, and held her hands.

"Not now, Rosemary," he said. "Don't think about it now."

Henri was still in the other room talking to the woman. He came out with some papers and pulled a chair over to sit next to Rosemary. He spoke in English. "You believe that you saw the body of the woman you knew as Shelley White?" His accent was strong but Rosemary could understand him well.

"Yes," answered Rosemary. "I have not seen her since she was fifteen years old. That is ten years ago. The face looked like her, but she had changed a lot. I needed to see the scar on her arm to be sure. You must understand. When I was ten years old my parents gave me a bicycle for my birthday. Shelley didn't have a bicycle, so she took my brother's bicycle. It was too big for her. She was so small! She fell off. If I had given her my bicycle, she wouldn't have had the accident. It's my fault!" Rosemary was talking very loudly. Tears were running down her face. "She hurt her arm badly. The scar is shaped like a V. Shelley said it was V for victory."

Henri spoke very quietly to Adam in French. Then Henri said, "Rosemary? Can you sign this please?"

He put a form and a pen on the coffee table in front of Rosemary. "Just sign here please."

Rosemary picked up the pen. She couldn't see what the form was. Her eyes were filled with tears. But she saw where Henri's finger was pointing and she wrote her name.

"You did well," said Adam. He helped Rosemary stand up. Then he put his arm around her and walked her back out of the building to the car. He helped her into the car and spoke to the driver. Very soon the car stopped outside a small hotel. Adam opened the door of the car. "Come on," he said. "You need to sleep." He took Rosemary's suitcase in one hand and put his other arm around her shoulders.

"Just walk," he said. "Only a few minutes, and you can sleep."

CHAPTER EIGHT

Rosemary woke up. The little bedroom was full of sunlight and smelt wonderful. It smelt of coffee and croissants and lavender. The narrow bed was soft and warm. Rosemary stretched. She felt wonderful. Then she realized she was still wearing the clothes she put on when she left her apartment in London on Saturday. Suddenly she felt dirty and unwashed. Her mouth was dry. She needed a drink and a shower.

She jumped out of the bed and looked for a bathroom. Just outside the bedroom was another door with a sign Salle de Bain. Rosemary used the bathroom, and drank some water from the basin tap. She went back and took clothes out of her suitcase. She grabbed her shower bag and a towel from the rack in the bedroom.

The bathroom was old but the water was hot. Rosemary was enjoying her shower when suddenly, the events of the past 36 hours came back into her mind.

Everything in Shelley's letter was a lie. She didn't work for a fashion magazine. She was a drug addict. She was living in someone else's apartment with no electricity or gas. The owner didn't know she was there.

She wanted me to come to Paris. Why? Then she was found dead by the river. Did someone kill her?

Rosemary wasn't enjoying her shower any more. She got out and dried herself quickly and got dressed. She threw her towels and dirty clothes on the floor of her bedroom, locked the door and hurried down the narrow stairs. At the bottom of the stairs, a young man in a police uniform was leaning against the wall.

"Bonjour, mademoiselle," he said. "The dining room is over there."

Rosemary entered the dining room. It was empty. On a side table was a pot of coffee, a big basket of croissants and smaller baskets with packets of butter and jam. Rosemary took a tray and served herself breakfast.

The young policeman entered the room and stood inside the door. *What's he doing here?* Rosemary wondered.

She sat at a small table. Even though she still felt very upset, the aromas from the coffee and croissants were so good that she drank her coffee very quickly and ate two croissants. She had just got up to get another cup of coffee when Adam walked in. He needed a shave and he hadn't changed his clothes.

He spoke briefly to the young policeman, who nodded and left the room. He came over to Rosemary at the side table, and said, "I think I'll join you. Can you pour me a cup?"

Back at Rosemary's table, Adam drank some of his coffee and then smiled at her. "How are you feeling today? Did you sleep well?"

"Yes, I slept very well. But I don't feel very good. I keep thinking about Shelley. I am also a little scared. Why did she want me to come here?"

Adam drank more of his coffee. He seemed to be thinking hard. He sighed. "I'll tell you as much as I can. Henri and I worked most of the night. We think we have most of the story, but it isn't nice. Shelley became a drug addict in Ireland. We don't know why she came to Paris, but she arrived about six months ago. She worked in a bar, and used all her money to buy drugs. We think she also stole things to get more money to buy drugs. Henri is checking now, but she probably took things like jewellery from the old lady's apartment where she was hiding. The nephew has come to Paris and he is trying to find what is missing from his aunt's apartment."

Rosemary's mouth was dry. She drank more coffee and said, "The jewellery box in the drawer was empty, but maybe the nephew did that."

"He says he did not go to the apartment after his aunt died. So maybe Shelley took the jewellery." Adam's voice was gentle.

"The members of the drug gang we arrested last night told us that Shelley stole drugs from them. Someone had seen Shelley. Maybe the young waiter from the café saw her and followed her. Or the concierge. Anyway, the gang found out where she was hiding. When they came to the apartment, they were looking for Shelley and of course, they wanted the drugs back."

"So they didn't kill Shelley?" Rosemary was surprised.

"No. She died from taking too many drugs. It is very sad. I'm sorry. I know she was your friend."

Rosemary stared at Adam. "Was she? Why did she want me to come here? She knew she was in danger. When I came I was in danger too! Why did she want that?"

Adam put his hand on top of Rosemary's. "There are two explanations. I don't know which one is true.

"Maybe Shelley was in trouble. She had no friends. She needed help. She hoped you would help her. Maybe she wanted to give up drugs…"

"And the other explanation?" asked Rosemary in a very small voice.

Adam held her hand tightly. "She had stolen a lot of drugs. The gang was looking for her. She needed to get out of Paris, and she needed to get the drugs out of Paris too. Maybe she thought she could hide the drugs in your suitcase or something. You would take them back to London, and she could get them later."

"I think the second story is probably true. If she wanted help, she would have told me. She wouldn't have put all those lies in her letter," Rosemary said sadly.

"Before I forget," Adam let go of her hand and reached into his jacket pocket. "The police have a copy of this. But you can have the original back." He handed Rosemary Shelley's letter.

"I don't want it." Rosemary was angry with Shelley.

"Maybe not now," said Adam. "But there are two things you must remember. Shelley had a hard life after she left England. She moved around a lot and was often very poor."

"Yes. Because she spent all her money on drugs!"

"But in all that time, she kept the photograph. The photograph of the two of you together. I think you should remember that."

Rosemary looked thoughtful. "That's true. Maybe I'll learn not to be so angry with her. Anyway, it's all over now and I can go home."

"Uh, but you aren't booked to go back until tomorrow."

"How do you know that?"

"When we were checking up on you, we looked at your flight

reservations."

"OK," said Rosemary slowly. "But I want to go home now!"

"Look," said Adam. "Just stay here for the day. Don't go out anywhere. Relax. You need the rest. And tonight I'll take you out somewhere very nice for dinner." He stood up, patted her on the head, and left the dining room.

Rosemary was very angry. *Who does he think he is? What does he think I am? I am not a child! I want to go home, and I will. They've caught the drug gang. Shelley is dead. I can't do anything for her. So I'll go back to London.*

CHAPTER NINE

Upstairs in her hotel room, Rosemary put everything back in her bag, and did her hair and makeup. She was ready to leave. She went downstairs to the front desk to pay her bill. The woman at the front desk said she didn't have to pay anything. It seemed that the police had an account with the hotel and they would pay for her room and breakfast.

Rosemary smiled and thanked the woman. Then she went out of the hotel and onto the street. She saw a sign for a Metro station and walked towards it.

I'll go out to the airport and change my flight. It might be expensive, but I want to be back in London. I want to be in my own apartment. I will have all day tomorrow to relax before I have to go back to work.

Back at the hotel, the young policeman was talking to the woman at the front desk.

"But where is she? Where is the tall blond English woman?"

"She left," replied the women. "She asked about her bill. I told her the police would pay. Then she left."

"Oh, no! My boss will be very angry! My job was to watch her and keep her safe!"

The woman laughed at him. "So why didn't you watch her?"

The young man went red. "I thought the English policeman was with her. I went to the bathroom. My stomach is upset. I ate some bad seafood last night. What am I going to do?"

"She might still be on the street," said the woman. "If you can't see her, you will have to call your boss."

He ran out of the hotel into the street, but he couldn't see Rosemary. She was in the Metro station, looking at the maps. He ran to the Metro station and was just in time to see Rosemary getting on a train.

He pulled out his phone and talked to his boss. "I'm sorry, boss. She escaped from the hotel. She got on the Metro at Faidherbe – Chaligny. The train is going to Gare du Nord. Yes, boss. I'll come back to headquarters now. I'm sorry."

Henri turned to Adam. "Your young woman has left the hotel. I guess she is going to the airport. Are you still sure she has nothing to do with the drugs? We only found a small amount in Shelley's handbag. I think Shelley hid the rest of the drugs somewhere. Maybe Rosemary found them in the apartment. Or maybe she already knew where they were."

Adam looked worried. "We checked her out very carefully. She has no connections with anyone who sells drugs, or uses drugs. I think Shelley planned to trick Rosemary into carrying the drugs for her, but I don't think Rosemary knew anything about it."

"So, shall we stop her at the airport and keep her in Paris?"

"We know that the rest of the drug gang are out there somewhere. We don't think they saw Rosemary, or know anything about her. But we can't be sure," answered Adam.

"I know what I want to do," said Henri. "I want to let her go back to London. I want to follow her. If the drug gang knows about her, they might be watching at the airport. We have a chance to see if anyone follows her. Then we can catch them!"

Adam was very unhappy. He was very attracted to Rosemary. He didn't want her to be in danger. But it was Henri's case and he knew he couldn't argue. "OK," he said. "But I want to be there."

"No problem," said Henri. "And please talk to the police in London. We want everyone watching to see if we can catch some more members of the gang."

And to keep Rosemary safe, said Adam to himself.

"Now please excuse me, I have work to do." Henri went out of the room.

CHAPTER TEN

Two hours later, Rosemary was at the airport. She went to the counter to change her ticket. It was easy. There were a lot of flights. She would have to wait almost three hours and she had to pay 100 euros extra, but she didn't care.

It's worth it. In about five hours I'll be home.

As she walked to the departure lounge, a smartly dressed woman with red hair looked at her. As Rosemary walked past, she pulled a smartphone out of her pocket and looked at a photograph. Then she made a call.

"I've seen her. She is taking a flight to London. You have the photograph? Be ready to follow her. I'll call you when I have the flight number. If you lose her, go to her apartment." The woman hurried after Rosemary.

The departure lounge was full, but Rosemary found a seat and sat down. In an office on the other side of the airport, Henri and Adam were watching the CCTV from the departure lounge.

"There she is!" Henri was excited. "And look! The woman with the red hair! That's Claude Maniere. We have thought for a long time that she is involved in the drug business here in Paris, and there she is!"

Adam was surprised. "But I was sure the members of the gang never saw Rosemary. Even if they saw her, how would they know to come here? How would they even know she was English?"

Henri laughed. "She is a classic English beauty, my friend. Her looks, her clothes! No one would think she was French!"

Adam was still puzzled. "But…."

Henri looked embarrassed. "Oh, Adam. We are good friends, and I know you like this woman very much. But I have a job to do. You remember we caught three members of the gang?"

Adam nodded.

"Well this morning, I called one of them to my office. I told him we had no reason to keep him. I gave his phone back to him. I had the papers about Rosemary on my desk. Pictures, her name, her address in London…I questioned him for a few minutes. I told him about Rosemary. Then I left the room. I left him alone with Rosemary's file. We watched him through a camera from outside. He looked at the papers. He took photographs with his phone. Then I came back and told him he was free to go. Of course he called the boss of the gang and told him, or maybe her, everything. So the gang have her picture and her address in London."

Adam was very angry! "Henri! They might kill her! That is terrible!"

Henri felt bad. "Yes. I know it is a risk. But I am a soldier. Yes, I say I am a policeman, but this is a war. So I don't feel bad about what I did."

Adam was still angry. "OK, I understand why. But if anything happens to her I will kill you!"

Henri laughed at Adam. "I knew you liked her. Maybe you are falling in love!"

CHAPTER ELEVEN

The flight back to London passed quickly. Rosemary was soon at the airport station waiting for a train to take her into central London. Although she didn't know it, four people on the platform were watching her carefully.

Three of them were policemen. Adam had called the drug squad in London and told them about Henri's plan. The policemen were there to make sure Rosemary was safe, but they were also watching to see if anyone was following her.

One of them was standing near the barrier, talking on his phone. "She got off the plane and is waiting for the train. I have no idea if anyone is following her, other than us! Two people who were on the same flight are also waiting for the train. There's a third guy, who was in the arrivals lounge. He walked out of the baggage claim area at the same time as Rosemary, but it might not mean anything. I took a picture of him. I'm sending it to you."

"Are you sure she's safe?" asked Adam.

"Yes, of course she's safe. Ron is standing next to her and Alyson is there too. When are you coming back to London?"

"I'm already back. I'm on my way from the airport now," answered Adam. "Thanks for the photograph, Noel. I don't recognize the man in the picture, but maybe Henri will. Send it to him."

The train pulled in. "Got to go, Adam. See you soon." Noel put his phone in his jacket pocket and hurried towards the train.

He got into the same carriage as Rosemary, but moved down to the other end. Rosemary found an empty seat and sat down.

"Mind if I sit here?" said a cheerful voice. The policewoman, Alyson, sat down next to her.

I don't know why she wants to sit next to me, when there are plenty of empty seats, thought Rosemary. But she didn't want to be rude, so she smiled, and moved her bag to make more room.

Rosemary got off the train at Piccadilly. Alyson and Ron followed close behind her. Noel got off the train, but he waited to see if the man he saw in the arrivals lounge got off too. He couldn't see him anywhere. He shrugged and looked for Alyson and Ron. He saw Rosemary

Just then a huge crowd of football fans blocked his view. There were hundreds of them. He pushed his way through the noisy crowd. His phone rang. "Yes?"

"It's me, Alyson. We've lost her."

"What! How?"

"Ron and I were right behind her when she went to change trains. We got to the ticket barrier at the same time, but those football fans pushed between us. She got through the barrier and onto the train. We couldn't catch the train. We'll take the next one. Do you know where she'll get off?"

"Uh, Kennington, I think. But there won't be another train for ten minutes or so. I'll call Adam."

Noel called Adam and told him what had happened. Adam was very angry and worried, but he knew it was not their fault. "I'll get the car to take me to Kennington Underground Station. Get a car to pick you up at Piccadilly, and go to her apartment. If anyone is following her, she could be in real danger."

Rosemary couldn't find a seat on the train. It was full of noisy football fans. She was tired when she got to Kennington Station. She pulled her suitcase along the platform. The elevators were full and there were a lot of people waiting.

Oh, dear! The stairs! All those steps! But I just want to get home.

She picked up her suitcase and started to climb the stairs slowly.

"Can I carry your bag for you?" A young man had come up behind her. He was wearing a baseball cap and a leather jacket. Rosemary thought she had seen him somewhere before. Maybe on the train?

She was going to say "Yes, please," when the young man smiled, showing a mouth of very dirty teeth, and reached out to take her suitcase. Rosemary changed her mind. She thought there was something a bit strange about him.

"No, thank you. I'm fine," she said. She started climbing again. The young man climbed the stairs too. He stayed very close to her. He was making her nervous.

At the top of the stairs, Rosemary hurried out on to the street. Her apartment was only five minutes' walk away, near the park. She looked back. The man from the stairs was walking behind her. He was talking on his phone. She walked faster.

I am being stupid. I have no reason to be frightened. But I am. I'll be OK as soon as I am inside my apartment. Don't look back! Just keep walking!

Finally, she reached her apartment. It was on the ground floor. She unlocked the door and pulled her suitcase inside. She locked the door behind her, and leant against it. She was shaking.

I'm safe now. I must calm down.

CHAPTER TWELVE

Adam was in a big black car. The driver was speeding through the streets of London, but he wasn't driving fast enough for Adam.

Noel called. "I will be at the apartment in about twenty minutes. Where are you?"

"About ten minutes from Kennington Station. Rosemary's train arrived there more than five minutes ago. That photograph of the man you sent me? Henri didn't know him, but our drug squad here in London did. He has connections with many gangs. I don't know where he is, and I am worried."

Rosemary had stopped shaking. She went into the kitchen to make a cup of tea. She sat down at the table with her tea.

What a weekend! I am so tired! But I guess when I think about it, it was a kind of adventure. And I met Adam. I should have stayed in Paris, and gone out to dinner with him. A date? Well, maybe. I think he liked me. But I've messed that up now by leaving. But he made me so angry....

Rosemary heard a noise outside the kitchen window. She looked up, and her heart stopped. It was the man who had followed her along the road. He smiled at her, and held up a knife. Rosemary was terrified. Then suddenly, she saw an arm go around the man's throat and he disappeared from sight. She ran to the window and looked out. A woman was holding him down on the ground. Rosemary was puzzled. It was the woman who sat next to her on the train between the airport and Piccadilly!

What is happening?

There was a loud banging on Rosemary's front door. "Ms

36

Moulton! Ms Rosemary Mouton! Police! Please open your door!"

She ran to her living room and looked out the window. The man banging on the door was wearing jeans and a leather jacket. Rosemary didn't plan to open the door.

Then a large black car stopped in the road, and Adam jumped out. He ran to the door, and talked to the man who was still knocking and shouting. The man nodded and disappeared. Adam knocked on the door.

"Rosemary! Please. Are you OK?"

Her legs were shaking, but she walked to the door and opened it. Adam threw his arms around her and put his face against her hair. "Thank God, you're OK. I have been so worried."

Rosemary leant against his chest. She felt safe. "Can I come inside?" Adam asked.

She laughed. "OK."

Adam let go of her, and she walked towards the kitchen. Adam closed the door and followed her. They sat down at the kitchen table and looked at each other.

Adam's phone rang. "Sorry, I have to answer this."

Rosemary got up and looked out the kitchen window. There was no one there. She thought Adam would like coffee so she took the grinder and the coffee pot out of the cupboard.

Adam got up and went to the front door. He opened it. Rosemary could hear him talking. Then he came back to the kitchen with three people. "Rosemary. These people are Alyson, Noel and Ron. They all work for the London drug squad. They were keeping you safe today."

Ron laughed. "Well, we were trying to! I'm sorry it didn't work out well."

"It was OK, in the end," said Noel. "We got the guy."

"I got him!" said Alyson. "Ron and I ran very fast from the station. We got here just in time. He would have attacked Rosemary if we had been only a few minutes later."

Adam looked upset. "I wanted to rescue Rosemary!"

"Well, you were late!" Alyson punched Adam on the arm. "I know you are crazy about her. Henri told me."

"Ooh, ooh," said Ron and Noel together. "Adam's in love!"

"Time for you guys to go," said Adam. He walked with them to the front door and came back alone. He sat down at the table again.

"But why did the English police follow me? Who was the man

with the knife? Nothing makes sense," said Rosemary.

Adam explained. "When you left the hotel this morning, Henri had two ideas. One idea was that you were part of Shelley's plan. You went to Paris to collect the drugs and keep them for her. The other idea was to use you to catch some more members of the drug gang. He wanted to follow you. I didn't like the plan, but I had to agree. Noel, Ron and Alyson are some of our best people. They watched you from the time you arrived in London. They promised me they would keep you safe, but of course they were looking to see if the drug gang were following you."

"But why would they follow me?" Rosemary didn't understand. "They never saw me. They didn't know who I was."

Adam was embarrassed. He explained what Henri had done. "He made sure the drug gang knew about you."

"The rat! I almost died of fright!"

"So did I. When I was driving through London, and it was taking so long, I realized that I have fallen in love with you."

Rosemary was still holding the coffee pot. She put it down, and looked at Adam. He got up from the table and walked around the table to Rosemary.

He put his arms around her. "If you had stayed in the hotel in Paris, none of this would have happened. We would be going out for a romantic dinner about now."

"Hmmm." Rosemary lifted her face, and Adam kissed her. "We could have dinner here. Do you like frozen pizza?"

THANK YOU

Thank you for reading I Need a Friend. (Word count: 11,679) We hope you enjoyed it.

If you would like to read more graded readers, please visit our website http://www.italkyoutalk.com

Other Level 3 graded readers include
A Dangerous Weekend
A Holiday to Remember
Akiko and Amy Part 1
Akiko and Amy Part 2
Akiko and Amy Part 3
Be My Valentine
Different Seas
Enjoy Your Business Trip
Enjoy Your Homestay
Old Jack's Ghost Stories from England (1)
Old Jack's Ghost Stories from England (2)
Old Jack's Ghost Stories from Ireland
Old Jack's Ghost Stories from Japan
Old Jack's Ghost Stories from Scotland
Old Jack's Ghost Stories from Wales
Party Time!
Stories for Christmas
The Curse

Together Again
Who is Holly?

ABOUT THE AUTHOR

I Talk You Talk Press is a Japan-based publisher of language textbooks, graded readers and language learning/teaching resources.

Our team is made up of highly experienced language teachers and translators, who have all studied at least one additional language to an advanced level.

This experience enables us to design our materials from the perspective of both the teacher and the learner. We consult with both teachers and language learners when designing our textbooks and graded readers, and test our materials extensively in the classroom before publication.

We are a fast-growing press, and currently publish graded readers for learners of English. We publish new graded readers monthly.

www.ingramcontent.com/pod-product-compliance
Lightning Source LLC
Chambersburg PA
CBHW022347040426
42449CB00006B/760